W9-DEZ-674

GO WEST!
Travel to the Wild Frontier

GO WEST WITH MERCHANTS AND TRADERS

Cynthia O'Brien

Crabtree Publishing Company
www.crabtreebooks.com

Crabtree Publishing Company
www.crabtreebooks.com

Author: Cynthia O'Brien

Consultant: Professor Patricia Loughlin,
     University of Central Oklahoma

Managing Editor: Tim Cooke

Designer: Lynne Lennon

Picture Manager: Sophie Mortimer

Design Manager: Keith Davis

Editorial Director: Lindsey Lowe

Project Coordinator: Kathy Middleton

Editor: Janine Deschenes

Proofreaders: Wendy Scavuzzo and Petrice Custance

Children's Publisher: Anne O'Daly

Production coordinator and Prepress techician: Tammy McGarr

Print coordinator: Katherine Bertie

Production coordinated by Brown Bear Books

Photographs:
Front Cover: **Getty Images:** br; **Topfoto:** The Granger Collection main, tr.

Interior: **Alamy:** Interfoto21, Lebrecht Music and arts 11t; **Corbis:** Lebrecht Music and Arts 16; **Graphic Stock Vintage:** 27l; **Library of Congress:** 4, 10, 12tl, 12br, 17b, 18b, 19, 28bl, 29; **Riverside Metropolitan Museum, Riverside, CA:** 18l; **Shutterstock:** 15b, Afroca Studio 22, AMC Photography 27tr, Andy Dean Photography 24inset, Dutch Scenery 20inset, Everett Historical 20r, 25, Nikitta 7tr, Joseph Sohm 13br; **Thinkstock:** Erick Isselée 26, istockphoto 5t; **Topfoto:** The Granger Collection 5b, 6, 7bl, 11b, 12-13t, 15, 17t, 23, 24tr, 28cr.

All other artwork and maps **Brown Bear Books Ltd.**

Brown Bear Books has made every attempt to contact the copyright holder. If you have any information please contact licensing@brownbearbooks.co.uk

---

Library and Archives Canada Cataloguing in Publication

O'Brien, Cynthia (Cynthia J.), author
     Go West with merchants and traders / Cynthia O'Brien.

(Go West! travel to the wild frontier)
Includes index.
Issued in print and electronic formats.
ISBN 978-0-7787-2326-4 (bound).--
ISBN 978-0-7787-2338-7 (paperback).--
ISBN 978-1-4271-1734-2 (html)

     1. Merchants--West (U.S.)--History--19th century--Juvenile literature. 2. Fur traders--West (U.S.)--History--19th century--Juvenile literature. 3. Frontier and pioneer life--West (U.S.)--Juvenile literature. I. Title.

F596.O37 2016   j978'.02   C2015-907970-5
                                         C2015-907971-3

Library of Congress Cataloging-in-Publication Data

Names: O'Brien, Cynthia (Cynthia J.) author
Title: Go West with merchants and traders / Cynthia O'Brien.
Description: New York : Crabtree Publishing, 2016. | Series: Go West! Travel to the wild frontier | Includes index. | Description based on print version record and CIP data provided by publisher; resource not viewed.
Identifiers: LCCN 2016001508 (print) | LCCN 2015049837 (ebook) | ISBN 9781427117342 (electronic HTML) | ISBN 9780778723264 (reinforced library binding : alk. paper) | ISBN 9780778723387 (pbk. : alk. paper)
Subjects: LCSH: West (U.S.)--History--Juvenile literature. | Merchants--West (U.S.)--History--19th century--Juvenile literature.
Classification: LCC F594 (print) | LCC F594 .O24 2016 (ebook) | DDC 978/.02--dc23
LC record available at http://lccn.loc.gov/2016001508

Crabtree Publishing Company

www.crabtreebooks.com   1-800-387-7650

Printed in Canada/022016/IH20151223

Published in Canada
Crabtree Publishing
616 Welland Ave.
St. Catharines, Ontario
L2M 5V6

Published in the United States
Crabtree Publishing
PMB 59051
350 Fifth Avenue, 59th Floor
New York, New York 10118

Published in the United Kingdom
Crabtree Publishing
Maritime House
Basin Road North, Hove
BN41 1WR

Published in Australia
Crabtree Publishing
3 Charles Street
Coburg North
VIC, 3058

CONTENTS

What Are the Prospects?

By 1848, the United States had gained control over Mexican and British territory in the West. Settlement soon followed—and more settlers meant more business opportunities.

EAST MEETS WEST

★ East supplies the West

★ West feeds the East

During the 1800s, **industry** grew quickly. In the East, manufacturers mass-produced goods in factories. Meanwhile, the West had many **natural resources**, such as minerals, timber, farmland, and oil. As settlers moved west, they began trading to supply eastern industries with materials. In turn, eastern factories made clothing, farming equipment, and other materials western settlers needed.

DID YOU KNOW?

The hunters who killed buffalo on the plains wanted the animals' skins. But US manufacturers soon realized that buffalo bones were also useful. They could be processed to make sugar or fertilizer. Manufacturers also ground up buffalo hoovess and horns to make glue.

The First Boom

★ Fur trade expands west

★ Trading posts open for business

The first valuable trade in the West was based on fur from beavers, otters, and seals. In 1670, Britain formed the Hudson's Bay Company to trade furs. It was the first company in North America. As the West was opened up, the company opened trading posts such as Fort Edmonton in Alberta, Canada. The trade involved First Nations and Europeans. In 1808, John Jacob Astor set up the American Fur Company. Astor established Astoria (right) in Oregon. It was the first permanent US settlement west of the Rocky Mountains.

Mountains of Metal

Above: Steam engines pulled long wagons full of borax from the bottom of Death Valley.

In 1848, the discovery of gold in California began a gold rush. Later, gold **prospectors** found rich deposits of silver in the Rockies. The West also had supplies of copper, lead, and zinc. A prospector in Death Valley found borax, a **mineral** used to make ceramics, glass, and detergent. These minerals were valuable for growing western industries. Western traders also made money selling them to eastern industries.

WHERE THE BUFFALO ROAM

★ **Wild beasts killed for hides**

★ **Hunters rake in money**

By the 1870s, buffalo hunting on the Great Plains was a popular sport among white Americans. It was also big business. Traders sent thousands of hides to cities in the East and to Europe. Manufacturers used the hides to make belts to drive machines in their factories. Train companies bought buffalo robes, or cured hides, to make seats for railcars. The US Army made coats out of buffalo hide for its soldiers. By the end of the century, the buffalo was almost extinct.

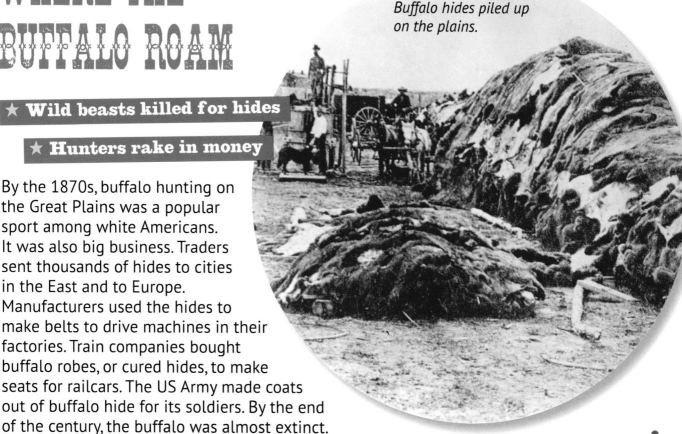

Buffalo hides piled up on the plains.

Meet the Folks

As settlers moved west during the 19th century, they needed goods and services. Merchants and traders started businesses to provide them, and many jobs were created.

THE MOUNTAIN MEN

★ **Fur trade comes to the West**

★ **Trading centers open**

In the early 1800s, the fur trade in the West expanded rapidly. Established firms such as the Hudson's Bay Company set up remote trading posts to buy furs from "**mountain men**" and Native Americans. Individuals, such as General William Ashley, a Missouri politician, saw opportunities to make money. In 1822, Ashley started the Rocky Mountain Fur Company. He hired 100 mountain men as trappers. Some, such as Joe Meek and Kit Carson, later became famous for guiding settlers to the West.

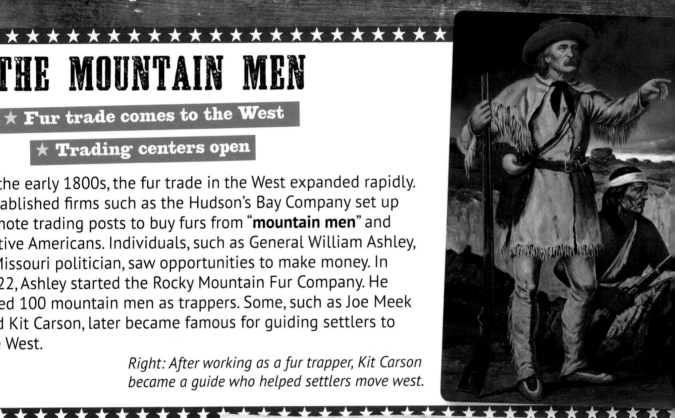

Right: After working as a fur trapper, Kit Carson became a guide who helped settlers move west.

MY WESTERN JOURNAL

You are the newspaper editor in town. Using information from this book, what kinds of stories do you think would interest your readers?

Give your reasons.

SITUATIONS VACANT

A Western town offers all kinds of jobs:

★ **SALOONKEEPER:** Must be prepared to break up bar fights. Late nights.

★ **NEWSPAPER EDITOR:** Good spelling useful— but not essential.

★ **STOREKEEPERS:** For grocers, outfitters, drug stores, and so on.

★ **HOTELIER:** To run anything from a boarding house to a luxury hotel.

★ **COOK:** Working in a hotel. Suitable for women.

★ **SCHOOLTEACHER:** Basic level only. Also suitable for women.

★ **BLACKSMITH:** To shoe horses and repair tools.

MULTI-TASKERS

★ Why do one job when you can do two?

★ Multiply your talents

In most towns, people did more than one job. The local furniture dealer also worked as the **mortician**. The local carpenter made the coffins. The newspaper editor sometimes acted as the town lawyer. The **blacksmith** sometimes ran the livery stable, where people kept their horses. Many hotels had their own restaurants run by the cook.

DID YOU KNOW?

Felix Gillet, a French immigrant, worked as a barber in Nevada City. He also worked as a fruit grower. In 1871, Gillet opened one of the first fruit nurseries in the West. He introduced strawberries and walnuts to California.

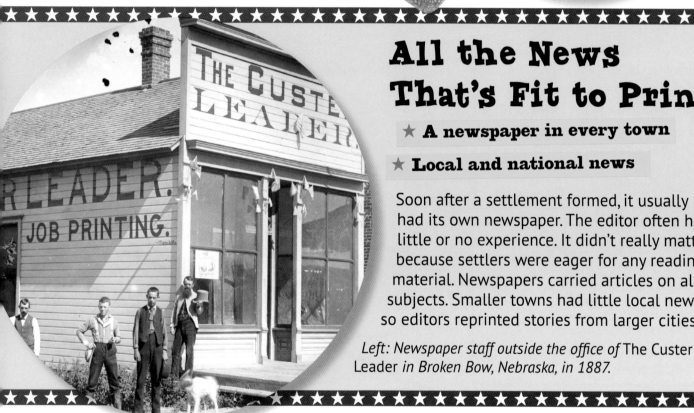

All the News That's Fit to Print

★ A newspaper in every town

★ Local and national news

Soon after a settlement formed, it usually had its own newspaper. The editor often had little or no experience. It didn't really matter because settlers were eager for any reading material. Newspapers carried articles on all subjects. Smaller towns had little local news, so editors reprinted stories from larger cities.

Left: Newspaper staff outside the office of The Custer Leader *in Broken Bow, Nebraska, in 1887.*

SHOPPING ON MAIN STREET

★ Town business booms

The first business in a new town was usually a general store or trading post. It sold everything settlers needed, from food to furniture. A saloon often opened at the same time. As the population grew, so did the businesses. There were specialty stores, such as bakeries, butcher shops, and drug stores. Banks followed, and a town photographer. Soon a main street could attract customers from in and out of town.

Where in the West?

Fort Edmonton
Fort Edmonton was built in central Alberta by the Hudson's Bay Company in 1795. The trading post marked the end of the Saskatchewan Trail from Red River Settlement (Winnipeg).

San Francisco
American settlers renamed the Mexican town of Yerba Buena as San Francisco in 1847. The following year, gold was found nearby and the United States won California from Mexico in the Mexican-American War. The sleepy port became the fastest-growing city in the United States.

Salt Lake City
The city, settled in 1847 by the Mormon leader Brigham Young, flourished. It was a home for Mormon settlers and a key trading post for settlers heading west.

Denver
Denver was settled in 1857 after a silver rush in the nearby Rocky Mountains. The city became a key supply and transportation hub between the eastern plains and the western mountains and coast.

Santa Fe
Santa Fe was the Mexican capital of New Mexico until American troops seized the town in the Mexican-American War (1846–1848). The town was transformed by the arrival of the railroad in 1880, and became the major trading center in the region.

UNITED STATES

San Francisco

Salt Lake City

Denver

Santa Fe

Trade grew up in the towns and cities of the West. Many settlements initially grew around railheads, general stores, and trading posts.

Key

———— Major railroads

● Towns with a population of over 5,000 inhabitants by 1895

CANADA

Toronto

Chicago

St. Louis

Fort Worth

St. Louis

St. Louis was the original departure point for settlers heading west. It later grew rich on trade with the West. Its specialties included brewing, flour milling, and meat processing. In the later decades of the 19th century, it was the fourth-biggest city in the United States.

Locator map

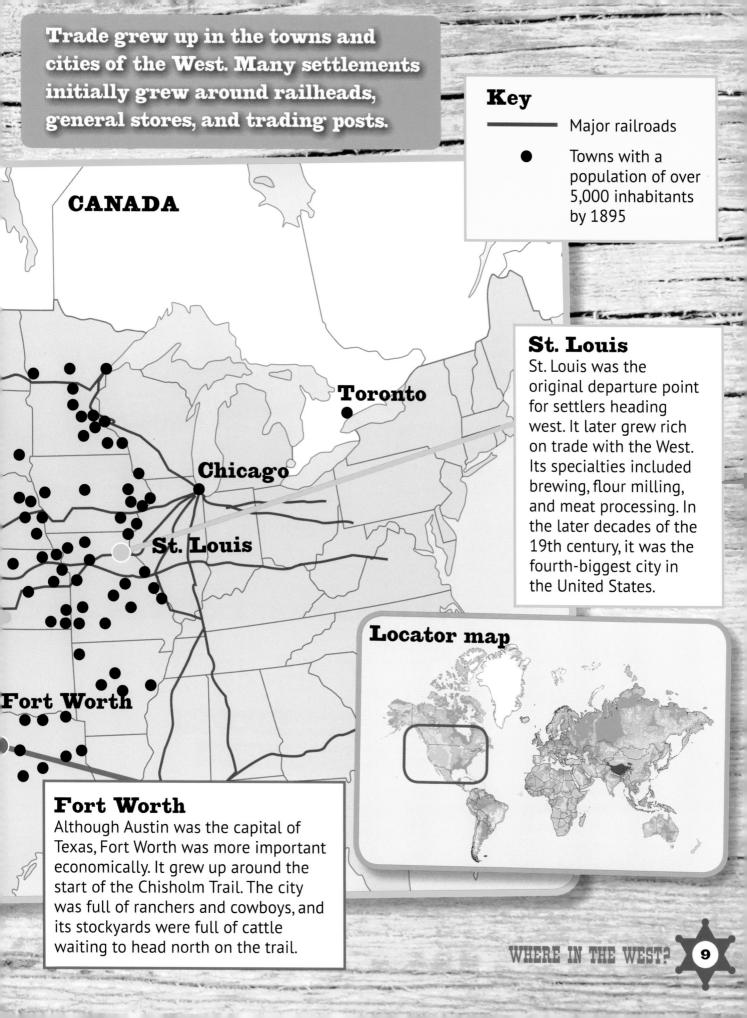

Fort Worth

Although Austin was the capital of Texas, Fort Worth was more important economically. It grew up around the start of the Chisholm Trail. The city was full of ranchers and cowboys, and its stockyards were full of cattle waiting to head north on the trail.

Let's Get Going

One of the challenges facing traders in the West was moving goods around. Before the railroads, cargo was shipped along rivers or over rugged trails.

Steamboats crowd the river bank in St. Louis.

MEET ME IN ST. LOUIS

★ **Capital of river transportation**

★ **Steamboats head west**

The Missouri River was the main water route to the West. The city of St. Louis is at the junction where the Missouri joins the Mississippi River, which leads south to Louisiana. The city became an important port. In the early 1800s, traders paddled or sailed boats on the rivers. Traveling upstream this way was difficult. That obstacle was overcome by the **steamboat.** It became the quickest and most reliable way to carry cargo and passengers.

DID YOU KNOW?

Russell, Majors and Waddell used up to 312 oxen to pull 26 wagons in an ox train. The oxen were guided by about 30 "bullwhackers" who walked alongside with their whips.

Strong as an Ox

★ **Ox trains take the weight**

★ **Stronger than horses**

Merchants used oxen to move heavy goods, or **freight**, around the West. They were cheaper to look after than horses and could pull heavier loads. In the early 1850s, Russell, Majors and Waddell was the largest freight company in the West. One of their most important contracts was transporting supplies to remote forts for the US Army.

PLENTY OF CHOICE

★ **A place to call home**

★ **Railroads lure farmers**

In the late 1860s, the railroad reached the West. Railroad companies sent agents to the East and to Europe to recruit new settlers. They particularly wanted farmers to move to the West. The railroads hoped that they would benefit from farmers who would use freight trains to ship their produce to markets in the East.

THE FINEST FARMING LANDS

CORN — COTTON — FRUITS & VEGETABLES

Above: An advertisement printed for a railroad company promises good farmland in the West.

Following the Boom

★ **Merchants chase opportunities**

★ **Cow towns welcome cowboys**

As the West boomed, money could be made wherever there were people. Merchants followed gold miners to California and lumber companies to the Pacific Coast. They also followed the railroad and the farmers who settled the West. Stops along the cattle trails could be profitable, as well. Cattle drives could take months, and trail drivers needed supplies along the way. Merchants sometimes sent gifts to the cowboys out on the trail to tempt them into town.

Left: Dodge City in Kansas grew as merchants and traders arrived to sell goods to cowboys guiding cattle along the Chisholm Trail, which ended there.

The Natural Setting

Most western trade was concentrated in settlements. Towns emerged at locations throughout the West and were settled for a variety of reasons.

★★★★★★★★★★★★★★★★★★★★★★★★★★★★★★★★★★★★

Location, Location, Location

★ **Travel by water …**

… or overland by wagon or train

Some towns in the West developed near rivers that were used for transportation. Kansas City (left) was settled next to the Missouri River. Other towns, such as Portland and Vancouver, were built on the Pacific Coast as ports. Others, such as Fort Boise, began as army posts on the wagon trails. By the late 1800s, railroads ran throughout the West. Cities such as Denver became transportation hubs between the West and the East.

★★★★★★★★★★★★★★★★★★★★★★★★★★★★★★★★★★★★

CITY BY THE BAY

★ **Gold fever strikes sleepy port**

In 1834, Mexicans built a trading post in California named Yerba Buena. It overlooked an outstanding natural harbor. In 1847, American settlers renamed the place San Francisco. Fewer than 500 people lived there. After gold was found in California in 1848, the population skyrocketed. By 1852, San Francisco had more than 30,000 people and was becoming a major city.

The former Mexican settlement, renamed San Francisco, became the major port for miners arriving during the Gold Rush in the late 1840s.

Settling New Territory

★ **Mining draws settlers**

In 1847, Brigham Young and 148 followers, called Mormons, settled near the Great Salt Lake in Utah. They named the town Salt Lake City. Although the town was remote and the region was dry and rocky, the population reached 20,000 people by 1880. The new arrivals included Mormons, and prospectors heading to the California goldfields. In the 1860s and 1870s, the growth of mining and the building of the Utah Central Railroad transformed Salt Lake City into a thriving urban center.

The main street of Salt Lake City in 1861, with a telegraph office (left) and a store.

DID YOU KNOW?

The first streets in Salt Lake City all measured 132 feet (40 m) across. That was just wide enough to allow a covered wagon and its team of four oxen to turn around.

GHOST TOWNS IN WAITING

★ **Here today, gone tomorrow**

★ **Miners abandon town sites**

Hundreds of western towns began as camps set up near "diggings," or mining areas. These areas were often in regions that did not suit settlement, such as mountains or deserts. For example, miners in Colorado settled Animas Forks high in the Rocky Mountains (right). Transportation to the town was very difficult, so the population never grew. Mining towns such as Barkerville, British Columbia, sprang up overnight while minerals were valuable. Once the minerals ran out, people simply left. Boomtowns became **ghost towns**, sometimes within just a few years.

Working with the Environment

Merchants in the West had to be creative. Among the many challenges they faced were isolated homesteads, transportation difficulties, and disappearing customers.

GOING WITH THE FLOW

★ **Follow the money**

★ **Moving around the West**

Although western towns grew quickly after the 1840s, they often disappeared just as quickly. Wherever there were miners or railroad builders, merchants opened temporary stores in wagons or tents to sell them supplies. When the miners or laborers moved on, the merchants simply packed up their stock and followed them to the next new settlement.

DID YOU KNOW?

Fires were a common hazard in western towns, which were largely built of wood. San Francisco alone had six major fires between 1849 and 1951.

$19.44

OUR REVOLVING AND RE-CLINING BARBERS' CHAIR
is first class in every way, but our price is very little more than is commonly asked for the old style r clining chair that does not revolve. **IT IS MADE OF OAK.** Legs are protected with brass mountings. All metallic parts are strong and well finished. We offer this chair in two styles, the cheapest having all the metal parts japan finished, the higher priced ones being heavily nickel plated. One is just as serviceable as the other, the only difference is in appearance. There is an old saying "appearance goes a great ways," and we know of no business where appearances go further than in the barber shop. If a barber wishes to get and keep the best trade his shop must be attractive. Our chairs and furniture will make an attractive shop.
No. 28R3610 Our Revolving and Re-clining Barbers' Chair, upholstered in mohair plush; colors, crimson, maroon, green or old gold. If color desired is not stated in order we make the selection. Complete as shown in illustration, except it has no scroll on the sides, being perfectly plain with metal parts japanned.
Price.................................$19.44
Weight, packed for shipment, about 210 pounds.
No. 28R3615 Same chair, with metal parts nickel plated. Price.........$21.60
No. 28R3620 Same chair, upholstered in leather, any color, japanned trimmings.
Price, each.......................$23.04
No. 28R3625 Same chair as above, with metal parts nickel plated.
Price, each.......................$25.20

Long-Distance Shopping

★ **Merchants go the extra mile**

★ **No need to leave the farm**

Settlers outside town sometimes found it difficult to buy what they needed—until the mail-order catalog arrived. This "Book of Bargains" offered everything from clothing to musical instruments, all shipped to the customer's door. One of the best-known mail-order companies was formed by Richard Sears and Alvah Roebuck. Sears, Roebuck and Co. produced its first catalog in 1894.

Left: Sears, Roebuck and Co. even sold equipment to traders in the West, such as this chair for a barber.

SEND IT EXPRESS!

★ **Wells Fargo takes over**

★ **Stageline from Kansas to San Francisco**

In the early days of the Gold Rush, the postal service in the West was slow and unreliable. In 1852, Henry Wells and William G. Fargo created Wells, Fargo & Co. to deliver money, gold, and silver in the West. Wells Fargo opened offices in cities, such as San Francisco, and in mining camps. After a bank crash in California in 1855, the company began to deliver mail between St. Louis and San Francisco. In 1858, Wells Fargo began the Overland Mail Company and took over major stagecoach lines.

Left: A stagecoach prepares to leave the Wells Fargo office in Virginia City, Nevada, in 1866.

Buy Local

★ **Eastern industry stops western progress**

When settlers arrived in the West in the mid-19th century, it still took a long time to ship goods from the cities of the East. Instead, western businesses manufactured goods locally. Most towns had a sawmill and a flourmill. The town carpenter made furniture and carriages. Shoemakers produced shoes and boots. Breweries supplied the saloons with beer. After 1869, however, the opening of the first transcontinental railroad made it easier to import cheaper goods from the East. Local businesses could not compete, and many closed down.

MY WESTERN JOURNAL

Imagine you lived in a Wild West town. Using information on these pages, decide what kind of business might be most profitable to start. Design an advertisement to promote your business and attract customers.

Making Money

Many products and services could be profitable in the West. Most were based on the region's natural resources, or the needs of the farmers and settlers who lived there.

★★

TRADE OFF

★ **Hides and tallow bound for Boston**

★ **Goods make their way west**

Before the Gold Rush, traders in California swapped cattle hides and **tallow** with eastern merchants. In return, merchants in the East gave the traders goods such as silks, coffee, and tools. Eastern manufacturers used the hides to make shoes, boots, and other leather goods. They used tallow to make candles and soap. After the railroads reached the West, the trade began again, this time using buffalo hides rather than cattle hides.

★★

No Vacancy

★ **A room for the night**

★ **From basic to luxury**

One way to make money in the West was by providing places for the thousands of new arrivals to stay. Every town had basic rooming and lodging houses. If a guest could not afford a room, some boarding houses had shared **dormitories**. If the beds were full, landlords rented out space on floors. Wealthier visitors stayed at hotels, which were luxurious—and expensive.

Right: The Palace Hotel in San Francisco had 755 large and luxurious rooms. It was the largest hotel in the West.

Farming the Plains

★ **Wheat spreads across the plains**

★ **Farming becomes big business**

In the 1800s, new machines changed the way farmers worked. Cyrus McCormick became wealthy after he invented a mechanical **reaper** in 1831. It made harvesting grain easier. John Deere invented a steel plow in 1837 that allowed farmers to cut through the tough soil of the plains. Deere's firm is still a leading maker of tractors. Wheat became an important crop. From 1866 to 1898, four times more wheat was harvested on the plains. Corporations created huge "bonanza" farms and made huge profits selling grain to the East.

Below: This advertisement for a McCormick reaper dates from 1875.

"OUR FIELD IS THE WORLD."

LIGHT DRAFT. SUPERIOR DESIGN.

CLEAN AND RAPID CUTTER.

McCORMICK IRON MOWER

McCormick Harvesting Machine Co., Chicago.

LET'S GO TO THE FAIR!

★ **Farmers put cattle on show**

★ **Fun for all!**

Agricultural fairs were popular events for western settlers. They were a social occasion, but they were also vital for business. Traders brought new farming equipment to display. Farmers and their families attended the fairs to learn about new developments and to meet their friends. State fairs became an annual event, attracting hundreds of people. Contests included plowing, and livestock and produce judging.

WEST IS BEST!

★ **"Dream" towns attract settlers**

★ **Merchants hope to make millions**

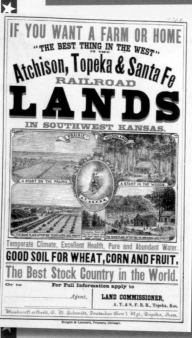

IF YOU WANT A FARM OR HOME
"THE BEST THING IN THE WEST"
Atchison, Topeka & Santa Fe
RAILROAD
LANDS
IN SOUTHWEST KANSAS.

PRAIRIE   WOODLAND

A START ON THE PRAIRIE.   A START IN THE WOODS.

THE SAME PLACE AFTER SIX YEARS WORK AND PROFIT   THE SAME PLACE AFTER TEN YEARS WORK AND PROFIT

Temperate Climate, Excellent Health, Pure and Abundant Water.
GOOD SOIL FOR WHEAT, CORN AND FRUIT.
The Best Stock Country in the World.
Or to   For Full Information apply to
Agent.   LAND COMMISSIONER,
A. T. & S. F. R. R., Topeka, Kas.

Railroad companies and merchants acquired huge areas of land. They divided the land into lots and set out to attract settlers. In Kansas, merchants eager for new customers created booklets that showed the thriving towns of Atchison and Sumner. In reality, Sumner had only a few buildings. It never grew. Today, it has just 500 inhabitants.

Friends and Neighbors

The West attracted people of all kinds. Some came from across the ocean and others from across the country. Most came in search of the chance to make their fortune or create a better life for themselves.

CLEANING UP

★ **Chinese immigrants start businesses**

★ **Range of services offered**

Thousands of Chinese **immigrants** arrived in the West during the Gold Rush. More arrived after 1865 to help build the transcontinental railroad. Other Chinese started businesses, such as restaurants. In 1851, Wah Lee opened the first Chinese laundry in San Francisco. By 1870, there were 2,000 Chinese laundries in the city (left) and many more elsewhere.

Witness to the West

★ **Tales of Virginia City**

★ **Writer pokes fun**

Samuel Clemens, better known as Mark Twain, started his career in 1862 as a newspaper reporter in Virginia City, Nevada. The city boomed when silver was found. By 1860, it had 42 stores and 42 saloons. Clemens, writing as Mark Twain, recorded life there in a comic style—he even invented stories to entertain his readers.

Right: This view of Virginia City shows the town in 1866.

MORMON MERCHANTS

★ **Travelers rest in Salt Lake City**

★ **Brigham Young rebels**

Salt Lake City was one of the most important destinations for travelers heading west. During the Gold Rush years, the Mormon settlers sold supplies to miners heading to California. There were few other stopping points, so Mormon merchants were able to charge high prices. The Mormon leader Brigham Young wanted to govern Utah Territory according to Mormon law. However, some Mormon practices were against US law, such as having more than one wife at the same time. The government refused to allow this and Young resigned, but the Mormon population kept growing. By 1900, there were 500 Mormon settlements in Utah.

Above: The Zion's Co-operative Mercantile Institution was opened by Brigham Young in Salt Lake City in 1868.

Army Forts

★ **Soldiers build posts on the frontier**

★ **Shelter and supplies**

The US Army established many forts along the frontier. Some outposts, such as Fort Laramie, Wyoming, were stopping points on the wagon trails. The fort provided protection and supplies for settlers and became a major trading post. The army also used the soldiers to keep the peace with Native peoples. The soldiers were a mixed group. Some had headed west after the Civil War (1861–1865). Others were immigrants and drifters.

DID YOU KNOW?

The Rocky Mountain Fur Company did not have trading posts. Instead, it held a yearly summer meeting for its trappers. The mountain men spent most of their time in the wilderness.

Hot Off the Telegraph

Advances in communications and transportation brought great changes to the West. As old ways disappeared, life became harder for some merchants and traders.

A Pony Express rider passes men setting up telegraph poles.

THE TELEGRAPH

★ **Pony Express out of date**

★ **New invention takes over**

In the early 1800s, express companies delivered letters to the West by coach or boat. In 1860, the Pony Express began. It used a relay of riders on horseback to provide faster communications. Less than two years later, it was replaced by the telegraph, which sent electrical signals much faster over wire. Telegraph wires were strung across the West. People sent messages down them in minutes. The Pony Express closed down.

MY WESTERN JOURNAL

Imagine that it is 1885, and you are a Chinese immigrant who owns a restaurant in the West. How would you feel about these laws? Write a letter home to your family in China describing your life in North America

No Chinese Allowed

★ **Laws obstruct Chinese immigration**

★ **Thousands refused citizenship**

Chinese immigrants helped build the West. But by the 1870s, many Americans resented the Chinese and blamed then for rising unemployment and low wages. In May 1882, the Chinese Exclusion Act halted Chinese immigration for ten years and banned existing Chinese residents from becoming US citizens. In 1885, the Canadian Chinese Immigration Act imposed a "head tax" on Chinese immigrants, making it too expensive for them to immigrate.

THE HUNT

In 1800, more than 60 million buffalo, or bison, lived on the plains. By the end of the 19th century, fewer than 300 remained. White hunters shot buffalo to sell their hides. Railroads also made money by organizing hunting parties as a form of sport. The hunters simply shot the buffalo from train windows. The disappearance of the buffalo had a devastating effect on Native peoples, who depended on buffalo for food, clothing, shelter, and trade.

Right: Terrified buffalo flee as hunters on a railroad open fire.

FARMERS UNITE

★ **Farmers form association**

★ **Montgomery Ward direct delivery**

Traders charged farmers in the West high prices, especially for goods from the East. Many farmers decided to work together to get better prices. They started an organization called the Grange, with local chapters all over the West. The Grange hired a Chicago salesman, Montgomery Ward, to buy goods directly from suppliers. This cut out expensive **middlemen**. In 1872, Ward moved a step further. He opened a mail-order business that still bears his name today.

DID YOU KNOW?

Montgomery Ward's first catalog in 1872 listed 163 items on one page. The goods were aimed mainly at farmers, and included threshers and farm equipment. By 1883, the catalog had grown to 240 pages and listed 10,000 items.

Bed and Board

Like other early settlers, merchants and traders faced harsh living conditions. However, success brought better food and higher standards of living.

TENT TOWNS

★ Trading under canvas

It did not take much to start a business in the West. The first merchants in California did their business in tents. They traded food, clothing, and tools for gold dust. As towns grew, merchants built wooden stores. The buildings were often basic, but the facades, or storefronts, were not. Owners built grand storefronts to help attract new customers. They also reassured existing customers that the storekeeper was running a dependable business.

DID YOU KNOW?

The first schools in the West were one-room buildings. Children in grades one through eight sat together. The youngest sat at the front, and boys and girls sat separately. Attendance was not regular. Farmers needed their children's help during planting and harvesting times.

What's on the Menu ?

★ Simple diet for most settlers

★ Oysters a popular choice

Homesteaders got food by hunting and farming. In towns, saloons and boarding houses offered dishes such as beans, beef, and bacon. Oysters were a special treat. Gold Rush miners invented the Hangtown Fry, an omelet made with bacon and oysters. Meanwhile, wealthy merchants enjoyed lavish dinners. They drank champagne as they ate roast meats or fish with rich sauces.

MENU
Try Our Western Favorites!

- ☞ Sourdough Bread
- ☞ Hangtown Fry
- ☞ Mutton or Curlew
- ☞ Omelets (Any Kind)
- ☞ Tinned Oysters
- ☞ Jarred Pickles
- ☞ Baked Macaroni
- ☞ Fresh Fruit (Sold Out!)
- ☞ Ice from Alaska
- ☞ Dried Apples

SCHOOLTEACHERS

★ **Women wanted for western schools**

★ **Harsh conditions and poor pay**

Before 1850, most teachers were male. Many were farmers who taught school in the winter. In 1852, Catharine Beecher formed the American Women's Educational Association. The association recruited young, single women to teach in frontier towns. Hundreds of women moved to the West to teach. Beecher believed that women did not need to be weak or passive, and that they should be encouraged to take a greater role in their communities.

Left: Catharine Beecher campaigned for improved education throughout the western territories.

City Life

★ **Stores and offices open in the West**

★ **People move to the city for work**

The first American settlers in the West lived on farms or in rural areas. As towns and cities grew, however, they began to attract newcomers. San Francisco and Denver became business centers. Meanwhile, the Union Pacific Railroad made its headquarters in Omaha, Nebraska. People worked at the city's meat packers and **stockyards**. Young women headed West to find work in stores, though they stopped working outside the home when they got married.

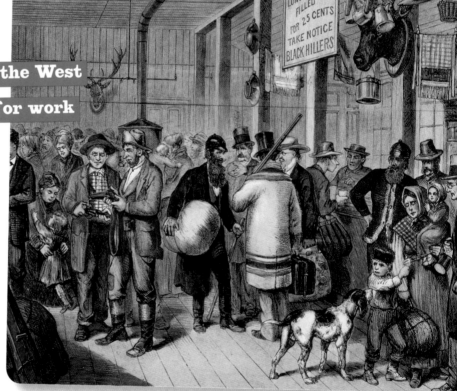

Above: The waiting room at the Union Pacific Railroad Depot in Omaha, Nebraska, in 1877.

Risks and Robbers

Setting up a business in the West could be risky for more than just financial reasons. Merchants and traders dealt with fierce competition, economic depression, and even bank robbers.

Money Market Panic

★ **Banks and businesses close**

★ **Railroads to blame**

Building railroads was expensive. The banker Jay Cooke **invested** in the railroads, but did not earn his money back. His bank closed in 1873, starting a financial panic. Savers lost their money and about 18,000 businesses closed in two years. People could not find jobs. In 1893, another panic began when two railroads closed. This time 15,000 businesses closed. This economic **depression** lasted until 1897.

Above: Jay Cooke invested more money in the Northern Pacific Railway than his bank actually had.

Everyone's a Winner ... Not!

★ **Merchants scramble to compete**

★ **Boomtown businesses fail**

For every merchant and trader who made a fortune in the West, hundreds more failed. Storekeepers in boomtowns lost all their customers when the population moved on. Boarding houses and restaurants often burned down. So many merchants arrived in Los Angeles to compete for business that they had to sleep in bathtubs when the hotel beds ran out! Meanwhile, town **speculators** lost out if they could not attract enough permanent settlers.

NO MONEY IN THE BANK

★ **Small banks struggle to continue**

★ **Bank robbers strike remote locations**

The first western banks were small. They could be risky places to keep money. Until 1863, banks were not subject to government rules, and some were corrupt. Crooked bankers set up "**wildcat banks**." They issued worthless money or stole savers' deposits. Bank robberies were another problem. The James–Younger Gang operated in Missouri. They stole more than $60,000 in their first robbery in 1866. Led by Jesse James, they robbed banks and trains for the next ten years.

Below: A sheriff's posse chases a gang who robbed a bank in Russellville, Kentucky, in 1868.

Losing Customers

★ **Miners move on**

★ **Business crumbles**

During the first years of the gold and silver rushes, miners arrived in the West by the thousands. Most were young, single men who had few possessions. They needed food, lodging, clothing, and mining equipment. This meant a sudden rise in business for local merchants, who could charge high prices for basic items. However, the miners often moved on as suddenly as they had arrived.

DID YOU KNOW?

Some new towns in the West printed their own banknotes, or money. Many traders worried that this local currency might lose its value. They preferred to accept US dollars or gold or silver.

Take It Easy

One way business entrepreneurs tried to make money in the West was by providing ways to pass the time. In general, entertainment was in short supply.

MUSIC TO THE EARS

★ **Audience cheers for Lotta!**

★ **Sing-along songs**

The West was full of music. In larger towns and cities, **entrepreneurs** put on musical performances in playhouses and theaters. During the Gold Rush years, Lotta Crabtree was the "San Francisco Favorite." She sang, danced, and acted. All kinds of entertainers made a living in the West, where audiences were often not very demanding. Song writers made money when people bought piano music so they could learn to play the latest songs.

POPULAR SONGS

These songs were popular in the West:

★ **"OH MY DARLING CLEMENTINE"**: This seems like a sad song about a miner's daughter who dies. Percy Montrose is said to have written it in 1884.

★ **"I'VE BEEN WORKING ON THE RAILROAD"**: This song written in about 1891 describes the back-breaking labor of railroad workers.

★ **"BUFFALO GALS"**: This song had many versions and many different titles.

Now for Something Completely Different!

DID YOU KNOW?

Phineas "PT" Barnum made a fortune from entertainment. With his partner, James Bailey, he organized variety acts and circuses to tour the West. The circus even included an elephant.

★ **Fun on the frontier**

One way businesspeople tried to attract customers was by offering something unusual. Entertainment was in short supply in the West, so any diversion from work was welcome. One saloonkeeper in Abilene, Kansas, kept a colony of prairie dogs in back of his saloon. Watching them kept his clients amused. Traveling circuses also brought exotic animals such as lions and elephants to town.

Get Your Head Examined!

★ **New "science" claims to have the answers**

One profitable business in the West was to give public talks. Visiting speakers gathered large audiences, and one of their most popular topics was phrenology. Supporters of phrenology thought it was possible to analyze someone's personality from the shape of his or her skull. Speakers spread the idea widely in the mid 1800s. By the end of the century, phrenology had been shown to be false and unreliable.

Right: Phrenologists believed different parts of the skull controlled the personality.

THE EARL AND THE GIRL
2 YEARS IN LONDON

EDDIE FOY.

THE ENTERTAINER

★ **New York comedian takes on the West**

★ **Musical comedy is a hit with the cowboys**

Eddie Foy Sr. was a stage comedian from New York City. He arrived in Dodge City, Kansas, in the early 1870s. The local cowboys were angry that Foy made fun of them in his act. They threatened to hang him. But Eddie and his stage partner, Jim Thompson, won the locals over with their musical comedy act. For three years, the pair sang, danced, and joked for audiences in Dodge City, Leadville, and Denver. Foy went back East and had seven children. In 1910, Foy and The Seven Little Foys started a new act, performing together as a family.

Left: This poster shows Eddie Foy in costume for the comedy play The Earl and the Girl *from 1905.*

Legacy of the West

The rush to gather valuable natural resources in the 19th century had a lasting impact on the development of the West. Its influence is still visible today.

THE RAILROAD BARONS

★ **Robber barons make fortunes ...**

... not just from railroads!

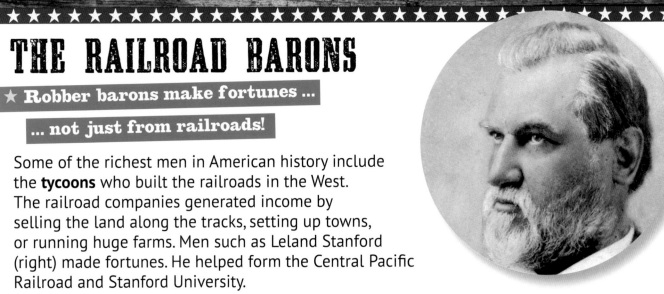

Some of the richest men in American history include the **tycoons** who built the railroads in the West. The railroad companies generated income by selling the land along the tracks, setting up towns, or running huge farms. Men such as Leland Stanford (right) made fortunes. He helped form the Central Pacific Railroad and Stanford University.

The view from Nob Hill looks out over the natural harbor of San Francisco Bay.

The Best Address

★ **If you've made it to Nob Hill ...**

★ **... you've made it to the top!**

The "Big Four" was the name given to the merchants who financed the construction of the Central Pacific Railroad in the 1860s. They were Leland Stanford, Collis P. Huntington, Mark Hopkins, and Charles Crocker. After they became rich, the four moved to San Francisco. They built luxury houses in one of the city's richest areas: Nob Hill.

Underground Wealth

★ **From rocky minerals ...**

... to "liquid gold"

Since the mid-19th century, minerals have been among the most valuable resources of the West. They included gold and silver, as well as coal, copper, borax, and lead. After the first oil was struck in the United States in 1859, prospectors began drilling for oil in the West. Large supplies were found in California in 1876, in Kansas in 1893, and in Texas in 1901.

DID YOU KNOW?

The men who made fortunes in the West are sometimes called "robber barons." Some people felt there was something unfair about the way they harvested natural resources.

LASTING LEGACIES

★ **LAZARD FRÈRES:** French brothers who sold dry goods to miners in California and used their wealth to open a bank.

★ **JAMES CLAIR FLOOD:** A saloonkeeper who sold mining stocks in Nevada.

★ **SIR GEORGE STEPHEN:** Cofounder and first president of the Canadian Pacific Railway.

★ **ADOLPHUS BUSCH:** Co-owned a brewery in St. Louis and started making Budweiser beer in 1876.

★ **JOHN D. ROCKEFELLER:** Formed Standard Oil in 1870 and became the richest man in the world at that time.

AUTO FAMILY

★ **Wheelbarrows to motorcars**

★ **Five brothers make fortunes**

From 1902 until 1966, Studebaker was one of the most famous names in automobiles. However, the firm's history had begun in 1852, when John M. Studebaker made wheelbarrows to sell to gold miners in California. In 1858, John and his brothers made their first wagon. Around half of all the wagons that settlers took across the continent were Studebakers. The firm began developing a "horseless carriage" in 1895 and made its first automobile in 1902.

Left: A Studebaker wagon from the 19th century, when the firm supplied wagons to the US Army.

GLOSSARY

blacksmith A person who shoes horses, and makes or repairs iron objects

depression A long period when economic activity is very slow

dormitories Large bedrooms in which a number of people all sleep

entrepreneurs People who take risks to set up businesses in the hopes of making money

freight Goods transported by truck, train, ship, or aircraft

ghost towns Towns that have been suddenly abandoned

immigrants People who move permanently to a new country or region

industry The part of an economy that is concerned with processing raw materials and manufacturing goods in factories.

invested Provided money to a business in the hope of a financial gain

middlemen People who buy goods from manufacturers and sell them to consumers

mineral A solid natural substance that has never been alive

mortician A person who prepares dead bodies for burial

mountain men Trappers and explorers who live in the wilderness

natural resources Substances that occur in nature that can be used to make more complex products

prospectors People who look for useful or valuable minerals

reaper A machine that cuts grain

speculators People who invest money in something that may or may not happen

steamboat A boat powered by a steam engine, usually through a large paddlewheel

stockyards Large yards with pens where livestock are kept before slaughter

tallow A hard substance made from animal fat

tycoons Powerful people in business or industry

wildcat banks Banks that are not official and that are commercially risky

---

1847

July 21: Mormon leader Brigham Young settles Salt Lake City in Utah.

January 24: Gold is discovered in California, sparking a Gold Rush.

1848

The first Chinese laundry is opened in San Francisco, in which the population skyrocketed thanks to the Gold Rush.

1851

1852

Wells, Fargo & Company open an express delivery service throughout the West. They later begin a stagecoach service.

Russell, Majors and Waddell start an overland freight business, using ox trains to carry goods to and from settlements in the West.

1855

1858

The Studebaker brothers build their first wagon. The wagons are widely used by settlers heading to the West.

ON THE WEB

http://www.thefurtrapper.com/Mountain_Men.htm
This site explores the fur trade, fur trappers, mountain men, trading forts, trading companies, William Ashley, and more.

http://www.legendsofamerica.com/we-towns.html
A page from Legends of America with links to many pages about towns and ghost towns of the West.

http://www.encyclopedia.chicagohistory.org/pages/779.html
A brief history of the mail-order business from the Encyclopedia of Chicago History.

http://www.ducksters.com/history/westward_expansion/daily_life_on_the_frontier.php
A page from Ducksters.com about daily life for settlers in the West.

BOOKS

Britton, Arthur K. *Life in the Wild West* (What You Didn't Know About History). Gareth Stevens Publishing, 2013.

Fleischman, Sid. *The Trouble Begins at 8: A Life of Mark Twain in the Wild, Wild West*. Greenwillow Books, 2008.

Hicks, Peter. *You Wouldn't Want to Live in a Wild West Town!* Franklin Watts, 2013.

Stein, Conrad R. *The Incredible Transcontinental Railroad* (Stories in American History). Enslow Publishing Inc, 2012.

The telegraph comes into use, replacing the Pony Express as the quickest way to send messages in the West.

Montgomery Ward publishes his first mail-order catalog for farmers.

May 6: The Chinese Exclusion Act prevents any more Chinese immigration to the United States.

Sears, Roebuck and Co. publish their first mail-order catalog.

1861   **1869**   **1872**   **1873**   **1882**   **1893**   **1894**

May 10: The first transatlantic railroad is completed at a ceremony at Promontory Point, Utah.

September 18: Jay Cooke's bank declares bankruptcy, causing a financial panic and a depression that lasts until 1879.

February 20: Bankruptcy of a railroad triggers another financial depression in the American economy.

INDEX